THIS BOOK BELONGS TO:

All Pages can be colored in for extra Fun!

I SPY With My Little Eye Something Starting With...

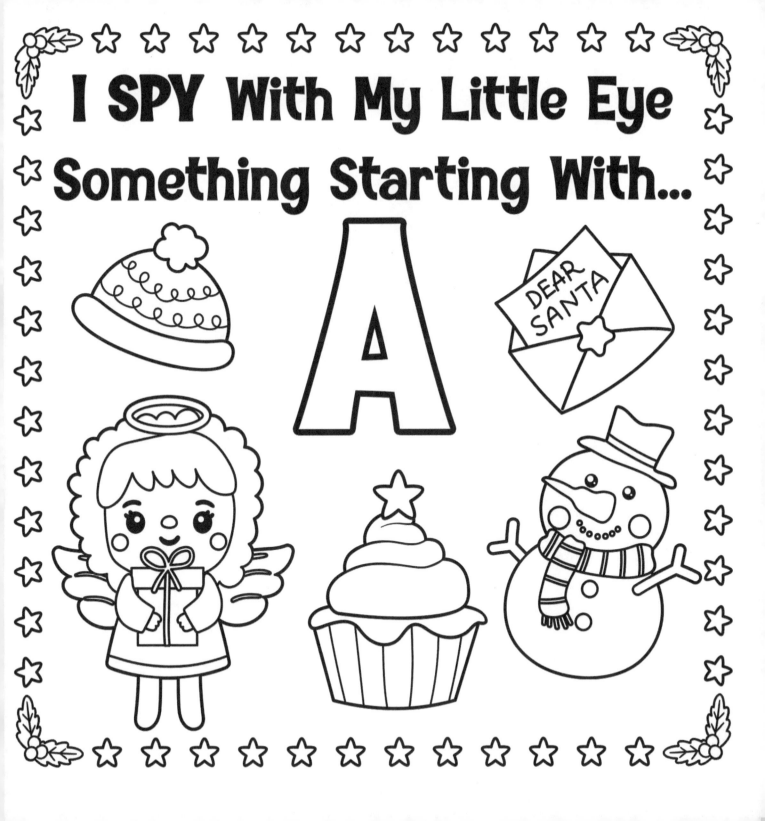

A

IS FOR

Angel

I SPY With My Little Eye
Something Starting With...

B
IS FOR
Bell

I SPY With My Little Eye Something Starting With...

C

IS FOR

Candy

I SPY With My Little Eye Something Starting With...

D IS FOR Dog

I SPY With My Little Eye Something Starting With...

E

IS FOR

Elf

I SPY With My Little Eye Something Starting With...

F IS FOR Fireplace

G

IS FOR

Gingerbread

I SPY With My Little Eye Something Starting With...

H

IS FOR

Hat

I SPY With My Little Eye Something Starting With...

J
IS FOR
Jingle Bell

I SPY With My Little Eye
Something Starting With...

I SPY With My Little Eye Something Starting With...

L
IS FOR

Lights

I SPY With My Little Eye Something Starting With...

M

IS FOR

Mittens

I SPY With My Little Eye Something Starting With...

N
IS FOR

Nutcracker

I SPY With My Little Eye
Something Starting With...

O
IS FOR

Ornament

I SPY With My Little Eye Something Starting With...

P

IS FOR

Penguin

I SPY With My Little Eye
Something Starting With...

Q

IS FOR

Queen

I SPY With My Little Eye Something Starting With...

R
IS FOR
Reindeer

I SPY With My Little Eye
Something Starting With...

S

IS FOR

Santa Claus

I SPY With My Little Eye
Something Starting With...

I SPY With My Little Eye Something Starting With...

U

IS FOR

Umbrella

I SPY With My Little Eye Something Starting With...

V
IS FOR
Vegetables

I SPY With My Little Eye Something Starting With...

W

IS FOR

Wreath

I SPY With My Little Eye
Something Starting With...

X

IS FOR

Xmas Tree

I SPY With My Little Eye
Something Starting With...

Y

IS FOR

Yule Log

I SPY With My Little Eye
Something Starting With...

O Z

Z IS FOR

Zero

Made in United States
Troutdale, OR
11/08/2024

24583155R00060